THE PATTON FAMILY

All members of the Patton family. George cherished them greatly, yet readily defied his father.
© The Huntington Library, Art Museum, and Botanical Gardens

George Smith Patton Junior was born on 11 November 1885 in the family estate in San Gabriel near Pasadena, in California. He was of a prestigious lineage of adventurers and soldiers on both sides of the family. After trading with the American Indians, his grandfather on his mother's side, Benjamin Davis Wilson (1811-1878) from Tennessee, became a trapper before moving to South California in the 1840s. He became a notable and was elected Mayor of Los Angeles in 1851, then Senator in 1869. He developed his ranch, Lake Vineyard, in the San Gabriel Valley, making his fortune from vineyards and citrus fruit plantations.

Portrait of Benjamin Davis Wilson by the artist Henry Augustus Loop. Oil on canvas.
© The Huntington Library, Art Museum, and Botanical Gardens

Hugh Mercer, who was killed during the Battle of Princeton, during the American Revolutionary War, was among Patton's ancestors. The very first Patton to head for America was Robert, who was born in Ayr, in Scotland. He left Glasgow to settle in Culpeper in Virginia around 1770. He married Mary Gordon Mercer, who gave him eight sons. Georgie's grandfather on his father's side, Colonel George Smith Patton I, commanded the 22nd Infantry Regiment during the American Civil War and took part in General Jubal Early's raid on Washington. He died on 25 September 1864 as a result of injuries sustained during the Third Battle of Winchester. The Confederate States Congress posthumously promoted him to the rank of Brigadier General. His widow Suzan then left the devastated State of Virginia to settle in California. Waller Tazewell Patton, his great-uncle, was killed 13 months

earlier, when in command of the 7th Virginia Infantry Regiment, during Pickett's Charge in Gettysburg. The two brothers are laid to rest together in Winchester. Another son, John Mercer Patton, survived the conflict, miraculously unscathed.

Young Georgie's father, George Smith Patton II, was an elegant, talented and literate southern gentleman. He graduated from the Virginia Military Institute (VMI), as had his father, to become a lawyer and, later, served as Los Angeles County District Attorney, before marrying Ruth Wilson. Nevertheless, 'Papa' - as his son called him - was obliged to resign from his position to take charge of the Wilsons' property assets.

▌*Portrait of Colonel George S. Patton in his Confederate States Army uniform, by the artist William D. Washington. Oil on canvas.*
© Virginia Military Institute Archives

▌*Young 'Georgie' with his mother and his sister, who was nicknamed 'Nita'.*
© The Huntington Library, Art Museum, and Botanical Gardens

A WARRIOR SOUL

George posing in uniform.
© The Huntington Library, Art Museum, and Botanical Gardens

Georgie and his young sister Anne, who was two years younger than him, grew up together on the family ranch. This extremely perky boy spent hours listening to his father read the Bible, works on the American wars and classics such as the *Iliad* or the *Odyssey* by Homer. He was brought up to worship his ancestors, the portraits of whom adorned the walls of the family home, developing a passion for the history of illustrious warlords, and a military vocation in the process. Behind the daredevil and skilled horseman, there was a capricious and even tyrannical young boy.

The Pattons with Ruth's sister, Annie, lived in San Marino, where their children George and Anne were born. In 1903, the Shorb estate was acquired by Henry E. Huntington, who appointed Patton as managing director of the ranch.
© The Huntington Library, Art Museum, and Botanical Gardens

Suffering from dyslexia, George Patton only attended the Pasadena boys' school from the age of 12. He worked hard to overcome his handicap, making use of his remarkable memory. Throughout his life, he maintained his own personal conception of spelling. As a teenager, Patton upheld old southern traditions as an athletic and well-educated young man. Patton decided to head for a military career. After a year spent at the Virginia

Sergeant Major Patton in dress uniform at West Point. A young man proud of his lineage.
© The Huntington Library, Art Museum, and Botanical Gardens

he married Beatrice Ayer, a gracious young lady with whom he had maintained written contact since their first encounter in Catalina during the summer of 1902. Assertedly ambitious, George S. Patton managed to obtain a posting at Fort Myer in Illinois, the nerve centre of the U.S. Army.

In 1912, he was selected to represent his nation at the Olympic Games in Stockholm. He took part in the modern pentathlon event. The highly demanding discipline was the perfect match for this accomplished sportsman. Unfortunately, during the pistol firing event, several 38-calibre bullets went straight through

Georgie proudly posing in his West Point cadet's uniform, with Nita, who is donning her shako and her long coat for the occasion.
© The Huntington Library, Art Museum, and Botanical Gardens

Military Institute, following in his father's and his grandfather's footsteps, he successfully passed the selection test to enter the prestigious United States Military Academy at West Point. Life as a cadet was very much to his liking. An accomplished sportsman, he regularly partook in horse riding, fencing and athletics, proving to be an outstanding marksman. Patton was a hard worker and he achieved excellent results. He came over as uncompromising and rather haughty with his fellow soldiers, in the belief that they were not of the same caste. His severity and exaggerated proclivity towards discipline embittered his relationship with them. Yet behind this 'hard to crack' shell, there was an emotional young man who regularly lacked self-confidence. Constantly self-doubting, he readily put himself in dangerous positions to test his courage and resistance. In 1909, he finally graduated in 46th position out of 103.

The young Second Lieutenant first joined the 15th Cavalry Regiment, based in Fort Sheridan (Illinois). Shortly afterwards,

Patton during a cross-country event at the Olympic Games in Stockholm. He mounted a Swedish horse, his own having suffered an injury. He nevertheless came in 6th. © Rights reserved

existing holes, and the judges counted them as failed shots. But he caught up, by beating Cléry, Europe's leading fencer. Of a total of 42 competitors, Patton came in 21st in shooting, 7th in swimming, 4th in fencing, 6th in riding, and 3rd in running. He finally finished 5th in the overall rank and first among non-Swedish competitors. On his way home, he stopped over at the Saumur cavalry school to perfect his skills with the elite in French cavalry. Thanks to this experience, he designed a new straight-blade sabre, adapted to suit the needs of the American cavalry. The M-1913 sabre was finally adopted and named after its creator. Patton returned to France for his honeymoon, during which he drafted a tactical manual on combat in the Normandy bocage. Then, over a later trip to France, Patton perfected his knowledge of the country. Upon his return to the United States, he trained at the Mounted Service School, in Fort Riley, where he was entrusted with sabre instruction for cavalry officers. Hence, he was the first to bear the title of master of arms.

The sabre Patton designed was lightweight, slender and balanced; however, its use proved to be ill-suited to cavalry charges which required heavier weapons for hitting with the tip and the edge.

© Rights reserved

M-1911 felt U.S. Army campaign hat. It was used for instruction up to 1941. © Private collection

When he left Fort Riley in 1915, the First World War had been raging throughout Europe for a year and Pancho Villa's revolutionary troops were defying Mexico's legal government and wreaking havoc along the border. Patton was transferred to Fort Bliss (Texas) to watch over Rio Grande. On 9 March 1916, the Mexican rebels entered New Mexico and attacked the town of Columbus. The ensuing action, which resulted in the death of several Americans, provoked an immediate reaction from Washington. Patton was successfully appointed aide-de-camp to General John J. Pershing, in command of the punitive expedition. Eager to confront, his hour of glory came during a motorised patrol. He intercepted Poncho Villa's men. After heroic combat, he managed to kill Julio Cárdenas, one of Villa's lieutenants. His story made the front page of the daily newspapers and the young soldier became a national hero. He was soon to be promoted to the rank of First Lieutenant.

Patton was inspired by Pershing's leadership style, the latter preferring strong and decisive action, remaining close to the front.
© Rights reserved

THE 'CHAMPION OF TANKS'

After his Mexican adventure, Patton returned to the monotonous life of the garrison. He was sent to Front Royal in Virginia to look after supplying horses to the U.S. Army.

He then considered leaving the U.S. Army and joining combat on the Old Continent. However, on 2 April 1917, President Wilson proclaimed the state of war between the United States and Germany. Pershing took command of the American Expeditionary Force (AEF), which was sent to fight in France. Once more, keen to join the conflict, Patton asked to be integrated within Pershing's staff. Promoted to the rank of Captain, he boarded for England on 28th May and arrived in Boulogne, along with Pershing's military staff, on 13th June. Weary with day-to-day paperwork, Patton asked to be posted in a combat unit. He developed an interest in tanks, a new and promising weapon, the routine use of which was not yet established. He was finally chosen to command the very first Tanks Corps unit. He trained with his French and British peers and toured battlefields to question tank crews. He overwhelmed his superiors with a deluge of manuals and reports. He studied the use of carrier pigeons and messengers for communication purposes and even went as far as designing a new uniform for tank crews.

Promoted to the rank of Major on 26 January 1918, Patton set up a tank school in Bourg-en-France, near Langres. His 500 men trained on French FT-17 tanks. Since he was the only officer to have any knowledge of this new weapon, he trained crews to work with the infantry. In August, he was appointed in charge of the 1st Provisional Tank Brigade (which was renamed the 304th Tank Brigade on 6 November 1918). After long months of training, the moment of truth finally came for Patton and his men.

▌ *The Distinguished Service Cross was awarded to those who had distinguished themselves through a heroic deed, yet that did not justify the Medal of Honor.* © Private collection

On 12 September 1918, Lieutenant Colonel Patton's unit was engaged in the offensive against the Saint-Mihiel salient to the east of Verdun. Amidst the tumult of the battle, the intrepid officer marched before his tanks as they advanced towards the village of Essey, in German hands. During the attack on Pannes, he mounted a tank to exhort his crews to advance even further, exposing themselves despite the danger. On 26th September, he led a group of tanks across eight kilometres inside the German lines during the Meuse-Argonne offensive. Patton was wounded in the leg near the village of Cheppy. Despite serious bleeding, he continued for an hour to dish out orders from a shell hole before being evacuated. It was to be his last day of combat in the Great War. Promoted Colonel, he left the military hospital on the day of the armistice, which coincided with his 33rd birthday. He was awarded the Distinguished Service Medal, the Distinguished Service Cross and the Purple Heart.

'I HAVE ALWAYS TALKED BLOOD AND MURDER AND AM LOOKED ON AS AN ADVOCATE OF CLOSE UP FIGHTING. I COULD NEVER LOOK MYSELF IN THE FACE IF I WAS A STAFF OFFICER AND COMPARATIVELY SAFE.'

Letter from George Patton to Beatrice, 23 December 1917

Patton posing in front of a Renault FT-17. This small French tank, of which around a thousand units were built under licence, was to form the backbone of the American armoured forces up to the early 1930s. © NARA

TIMES OF DOUBT

▌ *Christie TSE2 tank during a test phase. Equipped with a revolutionary suspension system and with rubber-coated wheels enabling them to advance at high speed without tracks, these tanks designed by J. Walter Christie were to leave a lasting mark on their time.* © Library of Congress

Once peace was restored, the officer's faith in the future of combat tanks was reinforced and he readily shared his views with another very promising officer with whom he had become acquainted, Dwight David Eisenhower. His experience was to serve the industrialist J.W. Christie in the design of a tank adapted for a war of movement. However, the American armed forces were mass demobilising and their budgets sustained drastic cuts. Patton's dream to, one day, see this weapon constitute a genuine independent force was fading.

The Tank Corps was disbanded in 1920 for economic reasons. With a heavy heart, Patton joined the cavalry. After having given him two daughters, his wife gave birth to their first and much hoped-for son in 1923. The following year, his hard work was rewarded. He graduated with merit from the Command and General Staff College in Fort Leavenworth (Kansas). After spending several months in

▌ *Colonel Patton during an inspection. He is wearing the Hawaiian Division insignia.* © NARA

various military staffs, he was temporarily affected to the General Staff Corps in Boston, Massachusetts, before being reposted to the Schofield Barracks in Honolulu in March 1925. His harsh tone and strong personality were behind him being recalled to Washington in May 1927. Patton worked on the concept of mechanised war. At the time, the United States was going through an extreme economic crisis and promotions were increasingly rare. In 1932, he studied at the Amy War College, a necessary step towards the coveted rank of general. Patton was, once more, transferred to Hawaii early 1935. As the years went by, his doubts in his future grew and his dreams of glory gradually withered. He drowned his sorrows in alcohol and had a brief affair with Jean Gordon, his 21-year-old niece, a fault that nearly cost him his marriage.

After spending three years at Fort Myer (Virginia), Patton was again sent to Hawaii. He was totally exasperated by inaction and frustration. In June 1937, the intrepid yachtsman travelled by boat to California. Incessantly pushing himself to the limit, he was seriously injured on several occasions. After a long period of convalescence, Colonel Patton was appointed in command of the 5th Cavalry Regiment, based in Fort Clark (Texas). A little later, he returned to Fort Myer, in command of the 3rd Cavalry Regiment. He then rubbed shoulders with General George C. Marshall, at the time Chief of Staff of the U.S. Army. The latter came to notice this somewhat nonconformist leader on the occasion of major manoeuvres.

▍*Insignia of the 24th Infantry Division.*
© Private collection

▍*Patton and his son George aboard the yacht Arcturus, off Hawaii, in 1937.*
© Rights reserved

'OLD BLOOD AND GUTS'

In September 1939, the guns were resounding throughout Europe. German tanks hurtled their way across the Polish plains, ringing the death knell of the mounted cavalry and the infantry masses. The *Blitzkrieg* literally stupefied the whole world. Perfectly aware of the threat, the United States chose to endow itself with a modern and entirely mechanised army. Marshall decided to create two armoured divisions. Patton, who was on good terms with him, tried to coax him to benefit his career. However, his cowboy manners and acquaintances in Republican Party circles were not necessarily to the liking of the powers that be in Washington. Patton chomped at the bit, as he waited impatiently for his country to enter the war.

M3 Lee medium tank. © U.S. Army

In July 1940, at the age of 55, Patton was finally appointed Brigadier General. However, Marshall had no intention of offering him a higher rank. He was appointed in command of the 2nd Armored Division, aka 'Hell on Wheels', stationed at Fort Benning (Georgia). His enlightened speeches galvanised his men. The armoured units demonstrated their superiority over the cavalry during large-scale manoeuvres. On 11 April 1941, he was awarded his second star and took command of the division. Patton cultivated his image, even making the front page of *Life* magazine. In just a few months, he transformed his unit, comprising 14,620 men, 390 tanks, 54 self-propelled guns and 3,630 vehicles, into a flexible military tool, capable of annihilating anything that crossed its path. He paid meticulous attention to communication and the chain of command. During large-scale manoeuvres organised in 1941, his unit proved its formidable efficacy.

Insignia of the 2nd U.S. Armored Division. © Private collection

Patton used an old cavalry tactic consisting in bypassing the enemy to attack from the rear. He launched the 2nd Armored Division 'blue columns' at full speed over a 650-kilometre raid across Texas, refuelling at local service stations. Patton had trained his units so well that, whenever a tank broke down, it took less than two hours for a repair unit to get it back on the road. The 'blue' columns bypassed the 'red' arrangement to reach, three days later, Barksdale airport in Shreveport, where Major General Benjamin Lear had set up the red army's headquarters. The latter complained that Patton had not stuck by the rules, eastern Texas being located outside the manoeuvre zone. But the Californian stuck to his guns and retorted, 'I am unaware of the existence of any rules in war.' Patton, who was one of the rising stars of the U.S. Army, was then appointed commander of the 1st Armored Corps.

▌*Major manoeuvres in Louisiana offered Patton an opportunity to flaunt his skills. Here, he is posing in front of his M-5 light command tank, easily recognisable thanks to its pennants and colourful markings.* © Fort Polk Museum

FROM MOROCCO TO SICILY

PATTON

▌*Patton preparing to leave* USS Augusta *to head for dry land aboard a Landing Craft Personnel. All the men that comprise his personal guard are armed with PM Thompson submachine guns.* © NARA

On 7 December 1941, Japanese planes bombarded Pearl Harbor, spurring the United States' entry into the war. Meanwhile in Libya, the British Army was at loggerheads with Rommel's *Afrikakorps* and needed reinforcements. Patton prepared his combat unit in the desert. To acclimatise and train them in conditions as close as possible to real life, he established the Desert Training Corps, in the centre of Mojave Desert. Patton was a tough but a fair leader.

After the Fall of Tobruk, the Allies decided to land in Morocco and Algeria to take the German and Italian troops from the rear. Appointed in command of ETOUSA, (European Theater of Operations U.S.

> 'I WANT MY MEN TO TAKE JUST AS ROUGH A BEATING AS I CAN GIVE THEM IN AS NEAR THE SITUATION THEY WILL HAVE IN NORTH AFRICA.'
>
> George S. Patton

Army), Eisenhower had three months to prepare the amphibious operation. He asked Patton to join him in Great Britain to take part in its planning. The Californian found himself in command of the Western Task Force that landed in Casablanca, in Morocco, whilst the rest of the expeditionary force set foot on Algerian soil. He disapproved Brigadier General Clark's appointment in command of the 2nd U.S. Corps, the latter being 10 years younger and, in Patton's opinion, unfit to command a unit that should rightfully have been his. Back in the United States, he supervised the boarding of his troops. On the night of 7 to 8 November 1942, the ships that comprised the Western Task Force crossed the Atlantic to arrive off the Moroccan coast. The assault was launched at dawn. Faithful to the Vichy regime, the French forces bitterly defended; however, Patton's troops reached their targets. On the 11th, Patton's 57th birthday, Casablanca surrendered. Over a thousand GIs were killed in Morocco.

The day after the operation, disillusion came for the Allies. After being chased out of Egypt and Libya, the *Afrikakorps* managed to re-establish positions in South Tunisia, with the VIII British Army at their heels. To the north, reinforcements came from Von Amin's divisions who held the 1st British Army at a distance. The 2nd Corps, commanded by the inexperienced General Lloyd Fredenhall, was bitterly overwhelmed by the *Afrikakorps* at the Kasserine Pass mid-February. Around 800 vehicles, including 180 tanks, and 6,300 men were lost. It was pure humiliation for the U.S. Army.

■ In Kasserine, the German tanks effortlessly overwhelmed the American M3 and M4 tanks, the latter being endowed with lesser firing power and inexperienced crews. © U.S. Army

▮ *Patton on the front page of* Look *magazine's 1 June 1943 issue.* © Private collection

Eisenhower summoned Patton to the rescue, placing him in command of the 2nd U.S. Corps, whilst Clark, his rival, had taken command of the 5th U.S. Army. Patton, who had remained restless and impatient in Morocco for two months, reorganised his ranks in just ten days. Discipline and training were, once more, the 2nd U.S. Corps' leitmotif. Patton put things back on an even keel, defeated the enemy at El-Guettar and joined forces with the British troops in Gafsa, obtaining his third star in the process. Tunisia fell into Allied hands on 7th May.

Sicily was but a stone's throw away. Despite appalling weather conditions, the British and American troops landed on the southern shores of the island on 10th July with the mission of capturing Messina. The 7th U.S. Army, now under Patton's command, set foot in the Gulf of Gela and warded off a powerful counter-attack by German armoured units. Further east, Montgomery's 8th British Army landed its troops in Pachino and the Gulf of Noto. With limited confidence in their allies' military capacity, the British only entrusted them with secondary targets. However, Blood and Guts was having none of it. With his customary spirit, he progressed rapidly to the north and northwest, whilst, to the

▮ *This column of Sherman tanks is waiting on the quayside in the port of Bizerte to board LSTs. 7 July 1943.* © NARA

▌ *Lieutenant General Patton landing on the beach in Gela in his inimitable attire.* © NARA

▌ *GIs in the city of Gela.* © NARA

> 'IT IS PERFECTLY FUTILE TO TRY TO COMFORT ANYONE FOR THE LOSS OF A SON, BUT I DO THINK THAT YOU SHOULD BE PROUD TO BE THE MOTHER OF ONE OF OUR HEROES WHO GAVE HIS LIFE IN THE DEFENSE OF HIS COUNTRY. I CAN NEVER LOOK ON ONE OF OUR WOUNDED SOLDIERS OR ON THE CORPSES OF ONE OF OUR MEN WITHOUT MY EYES FILLING WITH TEARS AND MY THROAT CHOKING UP, BUT WE SHOULD NOT, AS I OFTEN SAY, REGRET THAT SUCH MEN HAVE DIED, RATHER WE SHOULD THANK GOD THAT MEN LIKE THAT HAVE LIVED.'
>
> Letter addressed to Viola Reichstein, January 1944. Her son, Private Sam Reichstein, was killed near Salerno (Italy) after stepping on a mine on 21 September 1943.

west, Monty's men were at a standstill before Catania. Patton took control of Palermo on 22nd July and continued, determined to overtake the British. The Germans reinforced resistance as the Allies advanced towards Messina, sustaining increasingly heavy losses. The 3rd Infantry Division finally entered the town on 17th August. The enemy evacuated the island by sea and the British troops arrived a little later. Patton exulted… but his stubborn ways were to cause him some serious trouble.

▌ Lieutenant Colonel Lyle Bernard, commander of the 30th Infantry Regiment (3rd Infantry Division) speaking with Lieutenant General Patton near Brolo. © NARA

THE GENERAL'S BLUNDERS

The general's fiery spirit led him to commit acts that were to demean his reputation and be a hindrance to his career. On 14 July 1943, shortly after the capture of the Biscari airfield, Sergeant Horace T. West from the 45th Infantry Division's 180th Regimental Combat Team cold-bloodedly executed 35 Italians and two German war prisoners. Captain John T. Compton also had 36 Italians executed by his men. Notified of the affair, Patton declined any responsibility. The two incriminated soldiers claimed before the court-martial that they had followed orders not to take prisoners from their commanding general during a vehement speech given a month earlier. Patton was finally not held responsible for these two massacres.

> 'I TOLD BRADLEY THAT IT WAS PROBABLY AN EXAGGERATION, BUT IN ANY CASE TO TELL THE OFFICER TO CERTIFY THAT THE DEAD MEN WERE SNIPERS OR HAD ATTEMPTED TO ESCAPE OR SOMETHING, AS IT WOULD MAKE A STINK IN THE PRESS AND ALSO WOULD MAKE THE CIVILIANS MAD. ANYHOW, THEY ARE DEAD, SO NOTHING CAN BE DONE ABOUT IT.'
>
> George S. Patton

Generals Patton, Arnold and Mark Clark together in Italy on 8 December 1943. Patton was envious of Clark, commander of the 5th U.S. Army. © NARA

Patton in the company of Terry de la Mesa Allen and Ted Roosevelt, generals in command of the 1st Infantry Division, which was criticised for its lack of discipline. The Texan appreciated this hardened unit and demanded that Eisenhower authorise it to land in Gela. © NARA

On 22 July 1943, a cart drawn by two mules was blocking the progression of a tank column. Patton killed the animals with a revolver and had the cart pushed over the bridge. He used his crop to push away the Sicilian farmer. But our irascible general was to commit two far more serious indiscretions that caused him particular prejudice.

During a tour, Patton visited a 15th Evacuation Hospital aid station near Nicosia on 2 August 1943. He spoke to several wounded soldiers before noticing one man, seated on a stool. Private Charles H. Kuhl, from the 26th Infantry Regiment was suffering from severe dysentery and intense post-combat stress. Blood and Guts blew up and slapped the soldier with his gloves, before grabbing his collar and dragging him outside the tent, kicking him in the rear end and demanding he be immediately sent back to the front. A similar incident occurred

> 'THE OBJECT OF WAR IS NOT TO DIE FOR YOUR COUNTRY BUT TO MAKE THE OTHER BASTARD DIE FOR HIS.'
>
> George S. Patton

> 'WITH RESPECT TO PATTON, I DO NOT SEE HOW YOU COULD POSSIBLY SUBMIT A LIST FOR PERMANENT MAJOR GENERALS, ON COMBAT PERFORMANCE TO DATE, AND OMIT HIS NAME. HIS JOB OF REHABILITATING THE II CORPS IN TUNISIA WAS QUICKLY AND MAGNIFICENTLY DONE. BEYOND THIS, HIS LEADERSHIP OF THE SEVENTH ARMY WAS CLOSE TO THE BEST OF OUR CLASSIC EXAMPLES. IT IS POSSIBLE THAT IN THE FUTURE SOME ILL-ADVISED ACTION OF HIS MIGHT CAUSE YOU TO REGRET HIS PROMOTION. YOU KNOW HIS WEAKNESSES AS WELL AS HIS STRENGTH, BUT I AM CONFIDENT THAT I HAVE ELIMINATED SOME OF THE FORMER. HIS INTENSE LOYALTY TO YOU AND TO ME MAKES IT POSSIBLE FOR ME TO TREAT HIM MUCH MORE ROUGHLY THAN I COULD ANY OTHER SENIOR COMMANDER.'
>
> Letter from Eisenhower to Marshall, 6 September 1943

Pair of M7 binoculars.
© Private collection

at the 93rd Evacuation Hospital on 10th August. Patton set upon Private Paul G. Bennet from the 17th Field Artillery Regiment, who was suffering from shell shock. He slapped him twice in the face before threatening him with his revolver. This new incident spread like wildfire. Several reports reached Eisenhower's desk, resulting in an enquiry. Ike summoned Patton to publicly apologise, fiercely reprimanding him, whilst deploying his influence to ensure he did not lose his best military chief. The affair escalated and brought outrage throughout the United States. Patton was relieved of his command and, much to his despair, Lieutenant General Mark Clark took over operations in Italy. Yet, whilst tormented by the idea that others were fighting in his shoes, his superiors had not for as much forgotten him.

SHAPING HIS IMAGE

Patton cultivated his image as a hard-bitten war chief. He was and remained a horseman, as he readily reiterated. He was very rarely seen without his crop, his riding pants and boots. Blood and Guts donned his general's stars ostentatiously. On or close to the front, he wore his hard helmet, like any conscientious soldier, whereas, behind the lines, he preferred the forage cap. In 1944, he was accustomed to wearing the Hawley helmet with liner, painted with dark green lacquered paint and upon which his shimmering general's stars were affixed. However, the most singular item of his attire was undoubtedly the ivory stock revolver he constantly wore on his belt, like any worthy Texan. Contrary to common belief, he had several handguns which he regularly changed.

■ *Patton experienced a troublesome period after the regrettable Sicilian affairs. He felt betrayed by his peers and superiors, whilst Eisenhower did his best to preserve the man he considered to be his best war chief.*
© Life Picture Collection/Getty Images

FRANCE

Lieutenant General Patton and Major General Walter Robertson inspecting the troops from the 2nd Infantry Division in April 1944. © NARA

After long months of disgrace, Patton was finally entrusted with command of the 3rd U.S. Army. On 26 January 1944, he therefore landed in Great Britain. The SHAEF had been planning the invasion of continental Europe for months. Millions of men, tens of thousands of vehicles, planes and ships were gathered together across the British countryside and ports. To delude the Germans as to their true intentions, the Allies set up a formidable deception operation in which Patton played a major role: Quicksilver. The 1st U.S. Army Group (FUSAG), a phantom unit, was set up in Kent, in southeast England, immediately opposite Pas-de-Calais in France.

Patton, the most feared of all Allied generals, was placed in command,

Specialists from the 603rd Camouflage Engineer Battalion installing extremely realistic inflatable vehicles, aimed at deceiving the Luftwaffe reconnaissance planes. © Rights reserved

23

'YOU ARE NOT ALL GOING TO DIE. ONLY TWO PERCENT OF YOU RIGHT HERE TODAY WOULD BE KILLED IN A MAJOR BATTLE. DEATH MUST NOT BE FEARED. DEATH, IN TIME, COMES TO ALL MEN. EVERY MAN IS SCARED IN HIS FIRST ACTION. IF HE SAYS HE'S NOT, HE'S A GODDAMN LIAR. SOME MEN ARE COWARDS, BUT THEY FIGHT THE SAME AS THE BRAVE MEN OR THEY GET THE HELL SLAMMED OUT OF THEM WATCHING MEN FIGHT WHO ARE JUST AS SCARED AS THEY ARE. BUT THE REAL HERO IS THE MAN WHO FIGHTS EVEN THOUGH HE'S SCARED. SOME MEN WILL GET OVER THEIR FRIGHT IN A MINUTE UNDER FIRE. SOME TAKE AN HOUR. AND FOR SOME IT TAKES DAYS. BUT THE REAL MAN NEVER LETS HIS FEAR OF DEATH OVERPOWER HIS HONOR, HIS SENSE OF DUTY TO HIS COUNTRY, AND HIS INNATE MANHOOD. BATTLE IS THE MOST SIGNIFICANT COMPETITION IN WHICH A MAN CAN INDULGE. IT BRINGS OUT ALL THAT IS BEST AND IT REMOVES ALL THAT IS BASE. AMERICANS PRIDE THEMSELVES IN BEING HE MEN, AND THEY ARE HE MEN. [...] MY MEN DON'T DIG FOXHOLES. FOXHOLES ONLY SLOW UP AN OFFENSIVE. [...] EVERY SINGLE MAN IN THE ARMY PLAYS A VITAL ROLE. SO DON'T EVER LET UP. DON'T EVER THINK THAT YOUR JOB IS UNIMPORTANT. EVERY MAN DOES HIS JOB. EVERY MAN IS IMPORTANT. [...] WE HAVE THE BEST TEAM -WE HAVE THE FINEST FOOD AND EQUIPMENT, THE BEST SPIRIT AND THE BEST MEN IN THE WORLD.'

Extract from Patton's speech for the 3rd U.S. Army, 5 June 1644, England.

FUSAG insignia.
© Author's private collection

with the mission of deceiving the Germans on the true D-Day Landing site. Patton's participation in the actual invasion was never called into question. Fake tanks, trucks, planes and guns were installed throughout the region. Fake camps and intensive radio traffic simulated the presence of a sizeable unit. Attention to detail was such that even insignia were designed for the units supposed to be attached to the army group.

FUSAG's headquarters were set up in Wentworth, near Ascott. Remaining as discreet as possible, Patton supervised the preparation of the 3rd U.S. Army's 'Lucky Forward', scheduled to intervene during the second phase of the Normandy Landings. Alas, a public appearance on 25th April earned him further reproach from Eisenhower, which, this time, was to be of no consequence.

After waiting impatiently for several long weeks, Patton flew to Normandy on 6th July, in the company of his faithful Bull Terrier Willie. Lieutenant General Lesley J. McNair replaced him to ensure the further smooth running of Operation Quicksilver. Patton discreetly set up his command post in Néhou, in Normandy. He used a GMC truck equipped with a specially arranged cabin as his mobile headquarters. Blood and Guts prepared for his army to enter the fray.

The 1st U.S. Army was at a standstill in the Normandy bocage. The German

The M-1938 protective helmet made of fibre and issued to American tank crews was designed by the Rawlings Manufacturing Company, which also made American football helmets.
© Author's private collection

troops resisted every inch of ground, transforming each plot, each embankment into a battlefield in its own right. After the capture of Saint-Lô on 18th July, Bradley developed an offensive plan to break through the enemy lines. Poor weather conditions delayed the operation, baptised Cobra and finally launched on 25th July. To the south of the D900 road between Saint-Lô and Périers, the first German lines were annihilated under Allied bombs. The armoured units, divided into several Combat Commands, thrust into the breach and advanced southwards. As the 1st U.S. Army, now commanded by Hodges, headed for Villedieu-les-Poêles, Patton's 3rd U.S. Army took over operations along the coast

> 'I'M PROUD TO BE HERE TO FIGHT BESIDE YOU. NOW, LET'S CUT THE GUTS OUT OF THOSE KRAUTS AND GET THE HELL ON TO BERLIN. AND WHEN WE GET TO BERLIN, I AM GOING TO PERSONALLY SHOOT THAT PAPER-HANGING SON OF A BITCH JUST LIKE I WOULD A SNAKE.'
>
> Declaration by Patton upon his arrival in Normandy, 6 July 1944.

This M5 light tank from the 25th Cavalry Reconnaissance Squadron, 4th Armored Division, has been put out of action in the streets of Coutances, following the explosion of a mine. © NARA

An M18 Hellcat tank using its 76mm gun to clear a street in Brest in September 1944. © NARA

towards Avranches. General Grow's 6th Armored Division, 'Super Sixth', crossed Bréhal and Granville without stopping, whilst General Wood's 4th U.S. Armored Division, 'Breakthrough', made an in-depth advance, taking control of Coutances and Avranches.

On the following day, the Pontaubault Bridge over the River Sélune paved the way to Brittany for Middleton's VIII Corps, which reached Lorient and Brest in less than a week. After the failed German counter-attack in Mortain, the Americans entered Avranches on 31st July, to seize the miraculously intact Pontaubault Bridge the following day. In three days, 120,000 men and 10,000 vehicles crossed the River Sélune before fanning out from the opposite bank. France's liberation was in the making.

On 1 August 1944, Patton ordered Brigadier General Middleton, commander of the VIII Corps, to liberate Brittany and to take control of the port of Brest and Quiberon Bay. The 4th Armored Division reached the outskirts of Rennes, which was liberated on 4th August by the 8th Infantry Division. Vannes was freed the next day. The sheer speed of the American advance and the climate of insecurity maintained by the Breton 'maquis' resistance fighters prevented

> 'WHEN A MAN IS LYING IN A SHELL HOLE, IF HE JUST STAYS THERE ALL DAY, A BOCHE WILL GET HIM EVENTUALLY. THE HELL WITH THAT. MY MEN DON'T DIG FOXHOLES. I DON'T WANT THEM TO. FOXHOLES ONLY SLOW UP AN OFFENSIVE. KEEP MOVING. AND DON'T GIVE THE ENEMY TIME TO DIG ONE EITHER. WE'LL WIN THIS WAR, BUT WE'LL WIN IT ONLY BY FIGHTING AND SHOWING THE GERMANS THAT WE'VE GOT MORE GUTS THAN THEY HAVE OR EVER WILL HAVE.'
>
> Extract of a speech by Patton, England, June 1944

▌*Picture taken in Normandy of Patton, Bradley and Montgomery, seemingly relaxed. However, since Sicily, Blood and Guts was not particularly fond of the British general. In September, the situation was not to improve.* © NARA

Private Ernest A. Jenkins from New York, receiving the Silver Star from Patton for his bravery during the liberation of Châteaudun, France, 1944. © NARA

to push northwards and to trap the two German armies that were moving to the east. Major General Walton H. Walker's XX Corps, in charge of covering the 3rd Army's south flank, liberated Angers on the 10th and took Chartres on the 19th, before pushing on towards the Seine to establish bridgeheads.

Patton led his men at breakneck pace. They reached Verdun and the River Meuse on 30th August, but were brought to a standstill due to lack of fuel. Supplies were struggling to keep up, due to the increasingly long distance to be covered. Eisenhower had to choose between two possible tactics. Montgomery was keen to push on to Antwerp, then take up positions along the Ruhr, whilst Patton preferred to continue his advance and conquer before the enemy could reorganise. Much to his compatriot's dislike, Ike opted for the British plan. Unfortunately, operation Market Garden ended in dismal failure. The German forces exploited this convenient mishap to consolidate their positions in Lorraine, at a time when Patton was able to continue his advance towards the area.

The 3rd Army failed to quickly seal Nancy and Metz. After driving back a German armoured counter-attack by Arracourt, Patton took Nancy, 'the gateway to Germany', on 15th September after 10 days of combat; however, the fortified city of Metz resisted. The rain and the mud proved a genuine hindrance to Allied operations whilst the enemy demonstrated remarkable pugnacity. Patton was incensed when informed that he was relieved of command of the XV Corps; however, Metz finally fell on 21st November, enabling the American troops to progress towards Saarland, with the *Westwall* barely 60 kilometres away. The Battle of Lorraine was a costly one for Blood and Guts, with no less than 56,000 men lost, a gap that the replacement system was unable to fill.

the German troops from organising any form of line of defence. Two days later, the American tanks were at the gates of Lorient; however, the town was impossible to recapture. Meanwhile, the 6th Armored Division forged ahead towards Brest via Pontorson, bypassing Saint-Malo, still firmly in enemy hands. The 83rd Infantry Division was entrusted with the mission of liberating the citadel. Wood concentrated his forces around Brest, which was defended by some 40,000 Germans. By the time *Generalleutnant* Ramcke, in command of the occupied fortress, finally surrendered to the American troops on 17th September, the town and its port had been devastated. Ten thousand American soldiers were no longer fit for combat. The fortresses of Lorient and Saint-Nazaire held out until the end of the war.

Brigadier General Wade H. Haislip's XV Corps advanced southwards before swerving east to reach Mayenne and Laval on 5th August. Bradley in turn ordered

IN THE HEART OF THE REICH

Soldiers from the 1303rd Engineer Battalion's F Company posing on the bridge they have just built over the River Sauer to link Luxembourg and Germany. 10 February 1945. On another picture, the general poses with them. © NARA

The 3rd Army had no time to regain its breath. On 16th December, Hitler launched his major offensive in the West. In the Belgian Ardennes, the *panzers* thrust through the American lines and advanced towards the River Meuse. With the 101st Airborne Division surrounded in Bastogne, Eisenhower requested that all his commanders take that direction and put an end to the siege. George Patton replied that he could do the job. He wanted to use the same tactic as he had deployed in Louisiana in 1941. He had his army pivot northwards and counter-attack towards the town of Bastogne which he successfully liberated. Boosted by his success, he pushed on to Saint Vith.

The divisions finally succeeded in breaking through the *Westwall* defences and crossing the Eifel region. Koblenz was reached on 7 March 1945. Patton lost the race of the Rhine, Hodges outdistancing him to take the Ludendorff Bridge at Remagen. On their way up to Oppenheim, his divisions set foot on the opposite bank on the 22nd, one day ahead of Montgomery. Patton was promoted to the rank of General Four Stars on 14th April, in reward for his military success.

An American convoy advancing near Bastogne.
© NARA

Patton on a trip to his homeland, California, on 9 June 1945. The inhabitants of Los Angeles welcome him like a hero. © NARA

The 3rd Army attacked towards Kassel, Gotha and Fulda. Early April, advanced Allied units reached the Thuringian Forest. After reducing resistance in Mülhausen, Patton launched a large-scale offensive, deploying tanks over a 500 kilometre-long front. The U.S. columns entered Bohemia and crossed the Danube at Regensburg and Passau. On 5th May, they reached Linz, Austria, to join forces with the 3rd Ukrainian Front.

On 12 April 1945, Patton accompanied Eisenhower and Bradley to the Merkers mine, where the Nazis had concealed gold, liquid assets and works of art seized by the Third Reich, together with valuable objects stolen from POW camp victims. © NARA

Eisenhower ordered for Patton to stop in Pilsen and let the Red Army liberate Prague. When the Germans surrendered, his army took more prisoners than any other. But he was deeply moved by the destruction, civil exodus and the concentration camps. At the age of 60, Patton had no intention of leaving the battlefield. When Marshall rejected his request to go to the Pacific, he returned to his homeland for a long period of leave, to be welcomed like a hero.

Patton was named military governor of Bavaria and commanded occupation forces from his headquarters in Bad Tolz. This appointment marked a difficult period for Patton, now aware that he would no longer take part in any war. His remarks concerning denazification and his hatred for communists cost him his position. This cumbersome military leader contented himself with commanding the 15th Army, entrusted with writing the story of the conflict.

A FATEFUL END

The general's Cadillac just after the accident. © NARA

On Sunday 9 December 1945, Patton left his headquarters to hunt pheasant in a forest near Spire, a town in Rhineland-Palatinate. The following day, the five-star general was due to leave Europe to permanently return to the United States. Private Horace L. Woodring was at the wheel of the Cadillac Series 75 special limousine. Patton was seated to the rear with his Chief of Staff, Major General Hobart R. Gay on his left. The journey was going well when, at 11.45am, whilst approaching a bend, a GMC truck suddenly made an acute left turn without indicating. The collision was inevitable. Whilst the driver and Gay survived with only minor injuries, Patton, unable to anticipate the impact, was seriously wounded. Thrown forwards, the general's skull violently struck the dividing window. His cervical vertebrae were damaged and, although perfectly conscious, the officer was paralysed.

A rescue team rapidly took him to the military hospital in Heidelberg. Eminent specialists were rushed in and his wife Beatrice was by his bedside within two days. In both America and Europe, requests for news of his state of health flooded in. The diagnosis was not optimistic; his spinal cord had suffered damage. His neck was completely paralysed, and his respiratory and digestive functions impaired. Although perfectly aware of his condition, Patton never complained. For a week, he seemed to improve, before suddenly deteriorating due to pulmonary embolism. On 21st December, Blood and Guts passed away peacefully in his sleep. The following day, after a religious service, his coffin was transported by train to the Hamm war cemetery in Luxembourg. A number of dignitaries travelled to attend the ceremony. On 24 December 1945, a vibrant tribute was paid to this warlord of another age. Thousands flocked under the

▌ *Willie, his faithful companion, waiting by the luggage belonging to his master, whom he will never see again. In March 1944, Patton bought this bull terrier from a British woman whose husband, an RAF pilot, had been killed during a mission. After the general's death, Willie stayed with Beatrice and their daughters in California, to die in 1955, and be buried on the family estate in Green Meadows Farm.*
© NARA

pouring rain along the route taken by the funeral procession. Representatives from nine nations and the highest-ranking U.S. Army officers stationed in Europe followed his coffin. France and Belgium ensured the guard of honour. A French artillery battery fired a 17-shot salvo. After a brief religious service, George S. Patton Jr.'s coffin was lowered into the grave. As per tradition, his aide-de-camp, Sergeant William George Meeks handed over the Star-Spangled Banner that had covered his coffin to his widow. The general is laid to rest under a simple white cross amidst his men, as he had always wished, 'A soldier's body must be laid to rest, there where he fell.' Patton's grave was later moved to a more secluded spot in the cemetery to enable the many visitors to come and contemplate.

Beatrice died from a torn aorta at the age of 67, on 30 September 1953. She was cremated. Her wish to be buried by her husband's side was contrary to military regulations. In 1957, Ruth finally granted her mother's wishes, by spreading her ashes over her husband's grave, reuniting them for eternity.

▌ *The general's funeral. George Smith Patton IV, his son, took over. Also graduated from the United States Military Academy at West Point, he served in Korea and in Vietnam, to end his career at the rank of Major General.* © NARA